SASHA'S STORY

SASHA'S STORY

SURVIVING A SECRET HEALED AND STRONGER

LA'NEIKA BENBOW, LCSW, MFT

TATE PUBLISHING
AND ENTERPRISES, LLC

Published by Tate Publishing & Enterprises, LLC
127 E. Trade Center Terrace | Mustang, Oklahoma 73064 USA
1.888.361.9473 | www.tatepublishing.com

Tate Publishing is committed to excellence in the publishing industry. The company reflects the philosophy established by the founders, based on Psalm 68:11,

"The Lord gave the word and great was the company of those who published it."

Book design copyright © 2016 by Tate Publishing, LLC. All rights reserved.
Cover design by Joshua Rafols
Interior design by Manolito Bastasa
Edited by LaQuetta Benbow and N.H. Miles

Published in the United States of America

ISBN: 978-1-68207-234-9
1. Family & Relationships / Abuse / Domestic Partner Abuse
2. Family & Relationships / Marriage & Long Term Relationships
15.10.29

ACKNOWLEDGMENTS

First and foremost to God, who is my source and sole inspiration; I am blessed to have been chosen for this journey!

To my wonderful and precious daughter, you have given me the strength, courage, and vision to write this book. It is because of you that I continue to pursue life to the fullest. You are the reason that my life is so bright. Thank you for showing me how much God loves me, as he has shown his love for me through you. Remember that you are Awesome, Wonderfully and fearfully made! God blessed you in my womb, and greatness awaits you. I love you always!

To my parents, who have always been my greatest support and have loved me through it all. You have always provided me with care, compassion, and the greatest of all, love. You have cheered me on through the tough times and have always been proud of all my accomplishments. I am blessed that God chose you to be my parents. I could have never made it this far without you. I love you beyond words!

To my brother, whose laughter and silliness remind me that life doesn't have to be so serious. You are my big little brother, whom I am truly blessed to have. You have always had my back, and you mean more to me than words can describe. Our bond over the years has grown, and I am so proud of the man of God you are becoming. Love you!

To my sister, who gives me a listening ear and the best hugs. You have helped me travel through the rocky roads in my life and have reminded me to continue with the grace of God. You are a blessing to me more than you know, and at times, you have been the big sister. Our bond over the years has grown and strengthened in so many ways, and for that, I am truly thankful. You are becoming a great woman of God. Love you!

To my sister-in-law, you have given me insight and strength through many struggles. You are a blessed addition to our family and truly a sister to me. Your youthful wisdom has helped me in many ways, and for that, I am thankful. You have opened my eyes to the newness in my life, and for that, I am also thankful. Love you!

To my nephew, you are awesome and wonderful. You possess the name of greatness, and God has a plan for your life. Keep your head up and know that God will see you through everything. Focus on your future and know that "no weapon formed against you shall prosper!" Greatness awaits you. I love you always!

To my niece, you are an amazing little addition to our family. You are loved beyond words, and your life ahead is going to be amazing! Remember to love God, obey your parents, and walk in wisdom. Greatness awaits you. I love you always!

To my friends and family who have ministered to me through the years. I thank you for being there through my life experiences and this journey.

To all the Sashas near and far, let your trials and tribulations become the stepping stones others see in you that motivate them to continue. Remember, you are fearfully and wonderfully made with love! Through your struggles and your pains, remember that *you* are *survivors*!

God is our refuge and strength,
a very present help in trouble.

—Psalm 46:1

CONTENTS

PREFACE

So what do you think when you hear the words *domestic violence*? What do you feel? Do you cringe at the thought? Or do you simply think it's their issue, not mine? No matter the feeling you get, domestic violence is not as clear-cut as many believe. It is one of the deadliest silent killers and removes a person's ability to be heard and replaces it with fear. The physical harm many face, along with the mental and emotional trauma, can last for years and generations. The sad reality is that no one is truly immune to the potential of this happening to them or someone they love. Domestic violence has no age, race, or any other classification that makes it untouchable in your life or that of someone you may know. For this reason, *Sasha's Story* was written.

Sasha's Story is one that many share. It is one of secrets, guilt, shame, confusion, and Sasha's ultimate victory. It is the unlikely journey of a young girl who endured domestic violence, which followed her into her adulthood. Her thoughts and emotions are real and unimaginable to the mind of someone who feels they have been sheltered from the tragic pains of life. Having never thought her life would turn out this way, Sasha becomes depressed, has thoughts of suicide, and feels hopeless to the circumstances of life. *How could this be? What did I do to deserve this? Will it ever end?* These are the thoughts she ponders for years as she suffers through the pain she experiences. Overtime she gains strength and a voice, which moves her in a direction of empowerment toward a better life.

So what makes this book so different from others you may have read? Well, *Sasha's Story* is a journey that speaks to everyone involved. If you are in her shoes, I want you to know that there is hope. If you have people in your life that may be experiencing what you read, I want you to be able to understand it and know how to support them. And if you are the abuser, I want you to understand the impact on the lives affected by your actions—and that the love you are attempting to seek does not have to be reached in this manner.

The objective of this book is to bring to light the significance that domestic violence has on all those involved and to provide insight and additional understanding. It is also this book's intention to provide empowerment, education, and advocacy to those who are going or have gone through the difficulties of this situation.

As you read this book, I want you to become Sasha. Experience her thoughts and feelings so that it moves you to take a stand and make a difference. I would like for you to begin to identify the red flags and understand the pain experienced. If what you read exists in your life or in the life of someone you know or love, there is no true exemption from the aftermath this abuse may cause. However, the hope is that making it through this experience will help others and stop long-term repeated trauma. It is my prayer that the journey of Sasha will bring a change, creating healing for generations to come—let the journey begin!

I pray that as you read this book, you gain the strength needed to know that you are not alone, to know that you are worthy of a good life and that, although it may not feel like it, God loves you and is there for you as you endure this trial.

If you find yourself in this situation, admitting it is the first step in making any decisions about what you desire to do next.

It is not my recommendation or desire for you to read this book and then be put in harm's way. If you are in danger or in fear for your life, there are people who can help you. Information is available at the end of this book. You know your personal situation and its level of danger. Please be safe and seek the help you need.

If you are not in this situation but know of someone who may be, please proceed with caution. Each situation is different in nature, and some are more dangerous than others. Noticing the red flags and providing support is the first step. Be mindful that what you see is not always clearly visible to the person experiencing it. Stand strong with them until they get to the place where they can be reached.

1

The Beginning of Sasha's Journey: Youth and Dating

Omar

The Beginning of What I Could Not See

HI, MY NAME is Sasha Brogan, and I want to share the story of my journey with you. It's been a rough one—filled with some bumps, bruises, and cuts along the way. It has taken me a long time to be able to share this story, and I am glad that I now have the *strength* and the *voice* to do so.

My story starts when I was about twelve years old. I grew up middle-class with two loving parents, a brother, and a sister. We lived in a suburban neighborhood, full of multifamily homes clustered together. I was "well-rounded" and focused. My parents were always loving, hardworking, and supportive. What more could I ask? They always encouraged me to be strong, go after my dreams, and to never be pulled in by the environment that I live in. As I look back now, I see how much they tried to keep me from a life of heartache, tragedy, and disappointment. However, no matter how hard they tried, life happened to me anyway.

So where did your life go wrong, you ask? Well, as I continued to mature, I got to the awkward age and stage of dating and contemplating. You know, the age of acceptance and rejection, which was when life became interesting for me. This was the time in my life where my parents reminded me that I should not be dating until I was twenty-one! Boy, I wish I would have listened; maybe things would have turned out differently for me.

So yeah, back to my story. Omar was his name. He was muscular and had a chocolate complexion and the characteristics of a handsome model. He caught my eye a few times, but I never really gave him much thought. He was four years older than me. You know, I was only twelve, and my parents said, "You are not dating until you're twenty-one!" So when we first met, I was slightly bewildered as to what I should do.

I remember the day when we first met, out at the neighborhood pool. The guys were huddled by the side of the pool deck, laughing and chatting. Just then, my friends came over to me, whispering, "I think Omar likes you. He's been talking about you to his fellas." You know how it goes when you're a teen. The chitter-chatter and the giggling make you feel like love is truly in the air. My thoughts were, *Well, he is cute, but what would he see in me?* Just then, I watched as he walked toward me with his body-builder physique.

"Hey, Sasha, how you doing?" he said. Bashfully, I responded, "I am doing good." Awkwardly we both stood as he waited for me to continue the conversation I did not plan to have. Just then, I could hear my friends, off to my right, whispering and giggling. "Well, it's getting late I have to go now," I said as I began to head to the locker room to get my things and go home. "I'll walk you home," he responded.

Nervously I accepted the invitation. As we walked to the locker room, he began to ask me the "I want to get to know you" questions: What do you like to do? What's your favorite movie? You know, the awkward starter questions. Slightly stuttering, I replied with answers that I think at the time made sense.

Once I gathered my belongings, we began the two-block walk back to my house. Out of the corner of my eyes, I could see my friends smiling and giggling as they were confident that they did their job of getting us together. As we got closer, it seemed like hours before we would reach the cul-de-sac that my house was on. I felt as if I were perspiring; I was so nervous. Once we got to the corner, I thought, *I'm home, free!* But of course, he had to be a "gentleman" and escort me to my front door. *Will this night ever end?*

Quietness fell across the air as it felt like the world stood still. *This is the longest walk ever*, I thought. I could hear him talking to me, but all I could hear was the Charlie Brown *whomp, whomp, whomp, whomp, whomp.* Finally, we were at my porch. I'd never been so happy. Once we arrived, he walked me to the front door. *Don't you dare try to kiss me*, I thought. How would I explain any of this to my parents? But a gentleman he was. No advances made, no crossing the boundaries, respectful of me. *Wow.* "Have a good evening, and I will see you again," he said with a grin on his face. "Good night," I said, bashful but relieved.

When I walked in the house, I couldn't believe that I had been so bashful. Why didn't I talk to him? "Well, hopefully, I'll get another chance," I mumbled to myself while walking past my parents, who had been waiting in the living room for me. I said good-night and walked straight upstairs to my room. When I got there, I took a deep breath and took out the journal that I wrote in every night. I propped myself on the cushioned seat of my windowsill and looked out of the window; this helped me write better. As I gazed into the night sky to collect my thoughts from the evening, everything seemed to stand still. This was the night that started the journey of happiness and, unknown to me at the time, future tragedy. "Dear diary, today I met this guy Omar…"

So what happened next, you ask? Well, I got another chance, and the bashfulness eventually went away. Over time, Omar and I got to know each other; and yeah, I got past the awkwardness. We eventually started dating, and the true Omar began to show. However, because I was so wrapped up in the fog of lust at the time, I missed many of the red flags I should have caught. You know, people say, "Watch how your potential mate treats their parent" (guys, their moms; and women, their fathers) because that helps you see how they will treat you. Well, in many cases, that is very true!

Now, Omar treated his mother "okay." But looking back, I realized that he would show moments of disrespect and frustrated outburst from time to time. How did that relate to me, you ask? Well, I began to see some of those traits more and more as our relationship grew. There were periods of anger or frustration that made me feel like things may not be right. You see, growing up, I really never saw my parents get angry or upset with each other in my presence. Nor did I ever see them argue, so my expectations were based on my life growing up.

The first time I saw some of those traits I mentioned earlier was right before my thirteenth birthday. I remember the day Omar finally realized that I was younger than him. You see, I always looked older than my real age and was the more mentally mature type. I guess he just assumed we were the same age. However, we didn't go to the same school, so I'm not sure why he wasn't aware. The funny thing is that in all this time, he asked me every question except, How old are you?

As we stood in front of one of the neighborhood stores, I mentioned my birthday was coming soon. He looked at me and asked how old I was turning. "Thirteen!" I said, with a big grin on my face. I was finally going to be a teen. As I stood there looking into his face, it began to wrinkle; and a frown, followed by frustration and anger, came across. I felt a slight *fear* come over me. However, in my young age, I was not truly aware that, that was a red flag for future issues and turmoil. You see, no one ever explained to me that abuse was *not* just physical—that abuse starts out as *verbal*, *emotional*, or *mental* before it ever becomes physical.

So, Sasha, what happened next, you ask? Well, nothing that day. He was upset for a few minutes after finding out that I was only twelve. But with my birthday coming up real soon and turning thirteen, I guess he figured it was okay. I thought I would lose him before we even started. After dating for about a year or so, things began to change even more. We were now in the same school, and instead of things getting better, they got worse.

The first and only physical incident that occurred was one that will always be a part of this journey. As I look back now, I realize that once the physical abuse stopped, the verbal and mental abuse snuck in to take its place. I remember the feelings I had that day: *fear*, *confusion*, and *panic*. I don't remember how it started, but the trauma it caused replayed itself years later. You don't fully forget life's traumas, but you learn how to get through them. As I look back, I wish I had waited like my parents had told me to. Dating at a young age distorted life's focus for me.

So on this day, I remember going to Omar's house. His family was home. His mom was in the kitchen cooking dinner while his father was in the den with his two sisters and brother. We went to his room like we did most days and sat to watch television. I remember sitting and talking, and for some reason, he became upset with me. To this day, I really don't remember why. The next thing I knew, his strong thick fingers were wrapped around my throat, and I was pinned down on the bed. I remember him hovering over me with a big grin on his face as I gasped for air. What just happened? Why is he doing this? What did I do? At that moment, I felt a deadening silence come over me. Fear *paralyzed* me. I did not know what was going to happen next. I could hear his mom in the kitchen singing and smelled dinner cooking as I lay there, not knowing what to do. Do I scream? Will he stop?

Just then, he released his hold. As tears ran down my face, I scurried over to the head of the bed and cradled myself in the corner of the wall, afraid to move. As he approached me, still with a grin on his face, he said, "I was just playing." He reached to hug me, and I pulled back. *What just happened?* I repeated in my head over and over again. *Why did he do that?* Thoughts continued to run rampant through my head. *What just happened? Why did he do that?* Once the shock wore off, he reached out again in an attempt to hug me as if nothing had happened. I could still feel the warmth and strength of his hands squeezing my throat. "Are you okay?" he asked. "No. Why did you do that?" was my reply. "I'm sorry. I was only playing," was all he could respond. Too fearful to leave and not wanting to stay, I sat for a bit and then left to go home. I was still boggled by what had happened.

When I returned home, I was still shaken. Too embarrassed and not knowing what to say, I walked to my room in a daze. As I sat down, I reached for my journal next to the bed and began to write.

> Dear diary,
>
> Today something happened, and I'm confused. Omar and I were at his house today. His mom was in the kitchen, and his father and siblings were in another room. He put his hands around my throat

and choked me. I don't know what to make of that. I'm a little scared and shaken up. I can't tell my parents because I know that they will blow things out of proportion. I know that after a few days, we'll be fine. He said he was sorry, so I know he won't do it again. Maybe I'm just tripping. He did say that he was playing. Maybe I just need to lighten up, I don't know. I feel confused right now. These things only happen on TV. Well, let's see what happens next and go from there. Until tomorrow…

These were my thoughts at that time as the unbelief settled in. Several days passed, and things got better. He never tried to choke me again, but he began to make me feel less than or miniscule—to the point that I started to doubt myself. He would say things like, "You look nice, but where do you think you are going with that on?" He also began to treat me as if I didn't exist when his friends were around. I remember a few of his friends saying to me, "Why do you let him treat you this way?"

Well, by then, my mind had been distorted to think that everything was okay, and I had become accustomed to it. He created a new normal for me, and I'm not even sure how or when that happened. Lust is a terrible thing, and false love is even worse because it distorts your reality. It makes you think that things are okay when they really are not.

How could I be smart, well-rounded, all that stuff I mentioned at the beginning and still fall for this stuff? Well, I used to say the same about other people until I found myself in it. His charm, manipulation, and past hurts were matched with my loyalty, caring heart, and desire for the kind of love my parents had, this was a bad combination.

So time went on. Years passed, and through those years, the physical abuse never raised its ugly head again. However, the emotional and mental pain continued. I *knew* physical abuse was wrong, but no one talks about the mental and emotional abuse. So *no*, he never put his hands on me again, but he made me feel less than the person my parents were raising. He would yell at me and tell me I was stupid, dumb, and beautiful all in the same breath. He also began to become possessive, and my obligation and loyalty to him grew as my mind wrapped itself around the image of him and less around the image of myself.

During our relationship, I was so focused on creating us that I continued to miss all the things I should have seen. For instance, the fact that he was dating four other females while we were dating was something I should have paid attention to. What made it worse was that he convinced me that they were "just friends." My instincts knew better, but my mind told me otherwise. The manipulation, over time, distorted the rational and logical senses I had. And to be honest, I just didn't want to believe that, after almost four years of loyalty, I was being taken for granted. Other people came to me to tell me he was claiming to date others, and yet I still didn't want to believe. I realize now that was fear, hurt, and just nonsense. I deserved better.

However, at the time, all I could think was, *How could that be when I devoted all my time, energy, and love to him? We had been together for almost four years at this point.* You see, my mind-set even at a young age was to be committed to my mate, and I expected the same. As naive as that may sound, that was how I grew up. My parents and grandparents were all committed to each other, and that was what I desired. However, that desire blinded me from the truth, which was right in front of my face.

One day, the lightbulb just went off; and I remembered who I was and that, although I devoted much of my early youth to him, I deserved better. I had been misused, abused, and manipulated, and it was time for it to end. So one day, I said, "I HAVE HAD ENOUGH! I don't want to be with you anymore!" So that was it, right? He was okay with that because he had other girls he was messing with and we were just going to go our separate ways, right? Wrong!

You see, when I said, "I can't do this anymore," he pleaded with me and talked about how he "couldn't live without me"—yada, yada, yada. He even went as far as saying that he was going to "kill himself." Well, I couldn't have that on my hands. He seemed sincere, and I did love him, or so I thought. *Okay, maybe I'll give him another chance.* This relationship went on for about another year or so. Nothing really changed—just more lies and manipulations, incorporated with his fear of losing me although he continued to be with others. Looking back now, I remember that his life prior to me had its own secret traumas, which manifested in our relationship.

I had finally hit my rock bottom. I was reminded that I deserved better and that I could have it. So again, I said, "I HAVE HAD ENOUGH!" And again, he couldn't live without me and wanted to kill himself. However, by that time, I came to the realization that it was more manipulation. God forbid, if he did attempt to hurt himself, it wouldn't be because I ended the relationship. If he chose that road, it would have been because he realized truly what he did and how he treated me. But again, I mentioned that he did not have any desire to kill himself. It was more manipulation to keep me with him. He never hurt himself, but he did become very depressed. He began to realize that he took me for granted all those years and began to regret his actions. Leaving was hard to do but was eventually done.

We finally parted, a day that I never foresaw happening. But I felt free, and the *me* that I once knew resurfaced. We still remained in contact somewhat because we lived in the same area. But I started to move on with my life, and that experience made me stronger. After dating Omar, I met Kendell, and things began to look up.

Reflection

This was an unhealthy relationship, and many red flags were missed. Things missed were ongoing episodes of angry outburst, name-calling, the strangulation attempt, the guilt feelings (when he expressed killing himself), and the feelings of fear. As mentioned above, most see physical violence as the characteristic of a domestic relationship. You know, like Ike and Tina. So if you weren't being hit, the verbal and mental strains were not looked at very closely. However, as you can see, verbal and mental abuse is very real.

Many youth today are in relationships similar to Sasha's. The problem with dating too young is that you don't necessarily look at all you need to in order to pick a future mate. You don't think to look at life situations, circumstances, past trauma, or hurt. The focus of picking is solely on physical attraction. This was how I chose Omar, and I'm sure that's how he chose me. We dated for almost seven years, off and on, and I now realize that he had some life challenges he never properly coped with. He potentially mimicked what he may have seen in his own life growing up. People who are hurt and don't deal with it in a healthy way will carry it with them. Hurt people hurt others in their lives, and it's usually the ones closest to them. It wasn't until I got older that I realized that this was truly an abusive relationship.

Kendell

Hope for Tomorrow— the Light at the End of the Tunnel

So let's fast-forward. Some years have passed, and I was now eighteen. Omar and I have drifted and pretty much gone our separate ways. The relationship had an effect on me, but not truly significant, or so I thought. I was hurt by all the time lost and the nonsense that occurred, but I was able to move on and bounce back for the most part. By this time, I decided to refocus myself and prepare for a new year of school and eventually college.

So now, as an excited senior in high school and going forward with my life, I felt free! Is this the end of the story? Well, of course not. My journey was just beginning, and during this next part, God showed me that there can be real love in my life. This next journey was a joyful one, full of hope and promise. However, sadness and hurt followed as life did not seem to go in my favor.

Kendell Dalton was his name, and we met through our mutual friend, Nicole. Nicole and I are like sisters and, after all these years, continue to be the best of friends.

After looking at what I went through with Omar, Nicole felt like I needed someone in my life who would be that special someone for me, and that was where Kendell came in. My life changed at this point for the better. However, although there was not a significant effect, the relationship with Omar caused some reactions that I now see as I look back.

It was a beautiful evening in October when Kendell and I met. Nicole had invited me to a family masquerade ball, and being the matchmaker that she is, she arranged a double date. I remember getting to the ball—and no, this isn't Cinderella, but that night, I did meet my prince. I was not sure what to think or feel about meeting him, and I was very guarded. Not wanting to get my feelings hurt again and go through what I experienced with my past relationship, I wasn't very open. However, after being introduced to Kendell, I felt something was different about him. He was genuinely caring, honest, and a "true gentleman." *Wow*, I thought. In that one meeting, I realized that he was the opposite of Omar.

We lived in different towns and took things slow. As the days passed, we began to spend hours on the phone, talking as if we'd known each other all our lives. As we grew in our friendship, a dating relationship developed. I remember the first time he picked me up and took me out. I was amazed. A gentleman he was. I watched him open my car door before his and he also assisted me into the car. This was the experience I had desired. This was how my father treated me. I felt special, significant, and appreciated. Later in our relationship, he continued to find ways to let me know how special I was to him.

One significant memory was around Valentine's Day. I was still a senior in high school, and we had plans to go to dinner. However, on the day before Valentine's, I received a surprise. As I sat in class, I watched my guidance counselor come in with a bouquet of flowers. She stood and talked to the teacher for a bit before she announced, "Sasha, this was delivered for you." It was a beautiful bouquet of roses, and the card read something to the effect of, "I want you to know how special you are to me. I send this to you on this day because I want you to have your own moment and time to feel special." I smiled from ear to ear as others came to me, asking who I received my roses from. I did indeed feel special; no one had ever done that for me.

Through Kendell, I realized what "courting" really was. See, I had always heard of it, and no one really seemed to do it anymore, but I was being courted. He was seeking to get to know me, care for me, and love me genuinely. He never raised his voice at me, never put me down, and never made me feel less than. With that level of care, I was able to let my guard down and truly embrace what I desired. We continued on like this for some time and connected better than I had ever imagined. I felt respected and appreciated; he treated me like a queen.

As we grew in our friendship and relationship, we began to meet each other's families. I watched how he treated his mother, which was something I missed in my relationship prior. Kendell treated his mother with the utmost love and respect and never ceased to treat me the same. I met his parents and siblings, and all were loving and caring toward me. "This is the one I will marry," I began to say to myself. "He is everything that I've ever wanted." So the journey was over, and life changed for the good, so you would think. Well, things continued this way for a while; and I began to fall in love, truly, for the first time. However, I remember the day my dream was shattered.

It was a month or so before my prom, and I was getting excited to spend it with the one I loved. During one of our dates, I began to talk about the dress I wanted to wear, my hair, etc. Just then, he looked at me with a sad expression on his face. When I asked what was wrong, he said, "I won't be able to go." "Why?" I replied. The next few words changed my life forever: "I'm leaving for the army in two weeks." My life crashed at that moment. What had just happened? I had been through so much and finally felt like life was going in my direction, and now he was leaving. I was heartbroken. You see, prior to me, he had already enlisted, and I was not aware of that. We never thought that we would care for each other this much in this short period of time, but we did. So at that moment, life changed for both of us, and my straight path now had a detour.

Although difficult, we continued with our relationship, which was now very long distance. We talked on the phone almost every day when he could, sent letters, and had periodic visits when he was on leave, which seemed very seldom. We continued to desire to be together, and to some degree, the distance grew us stronger. However, ultimately, the military life drew us further apart due to the continuous reenlisting and never being able to see each other. We continued this way for almost three and a half years, trying not to let this stand in our way.

Over time, things just never seemed to get to the point that I had desired for them to be. Although the love was there, the focus for us to be more never seemed to come. Our lives at this time began to go in different directions and brought the greatest pain. His desire for me not to wait for him or experience potential loss of him did not match with my desire and longing to be with him. Coming together again just didn't seem possible, and we slowly drifted apart. Although we stayed in touch and remained the best of friends, we started to date other people.

For me, this was far and few in between. My trust in love, safety, and security with a future mate was slowly shattering over time. On one hand, my relationship with

Omar was a disaster, and I was glad to get rid of it. On the other hand, my relationship with Kendell was one that I could see myself in for life, and that just ended. Will I ever get this right? I began to wonder if I would ever get to that point of receiving the love and commitment I was seeking. By this time, I was in my senior year of college and decided that I was just going to focus on me. I decided to keep myself occupied, focusing even more on my studies, spending time with friends, working, and becoming more involved in campus activities.

So what does this have to do with domestic violence, you ask? Well, the journeys we take are both good and bad. Some of the hurts, pains, or disappointments we experience may guide us in the wrong direction later on. This part of my journey gave me hope but was part of the detour I faced later on. I went from disappointment with Omar to both happiness and sadness with Kendell. Life at this point just didn't make sense. Moving on was not easy at this time, and I wasn't seeking to truly be with anyone. I had friends to be around, and that was good enough. I was guarded again, and my heart was somewhat shattered yet still hopeful that things would turn around with Kendell, although they never did.

I felt lost and was seeking some resolve to my emotional pain. It was at this time in my life that I started to seek a more spiritual connection, and instead of focusing on others, I began to focus on God. This brought some healing and comfort in knowing that life would continue for me. The relationship I began to build was what brought me through the next phase of life. It is through my relationship with God that I was able to endure the next chapter of my life.

Reflection

All relationships bring an opportunity to learn and grow. My relationship with Kendell was a healthy one but ultimately did not work because of our own life's choices and focus at the time. I was ready, and he was not. We were both hurt through this process, and at least for me, I know it had a lasting effect. Being hurt in one relationship and then not getting the desired results in another can begin to taint a person's perspective on love in their lives. In the long run, this can lead to bad choices down the line. Holding on to just any kind of love because you feel like you won't be able to have it sets you up for a relationship built on fear.

2

Marriage

Yea though I walk through the valley of the Shadow of death, I shall Fear no evil for thou art with me.

—Psalm 23:4

Otis

How We met

So as I mentioned, a few years passed, and I was now twenty-two years old and finishing college. Kendell and I remained friends and in contact with each other over the years but never came together again. The military was his focus, and I respected that. So with my heart trying to get back on track, my focus turned from man to God. I began to seek a difference in my life, and building my relationship with God was becoming more and more important to me. In the midst of me regaining focus, I met Otis.

Otis Garret and I met at a party while I was in college. He went to a nearby school, and we just happened to cross paths. I had heard about him, and some things I heard were good and some not as favorable. I wasn't looking to get into another relationship at the time he approached me, and it pretty much stayed that way. I was guarded and didn't really give him a second thought. I noticed him noticing me a few times during the party and just made a mental note. One day, while I was traveling back to school, he just happened to be on the train with me.

"Hi, Sasha," he said. "Can I sit next to you?" In my mind, I said no, but I tried not to be rude. "Sure," I said as I thought about the almost twelve-hour ride I had to take. I just wanted to relax, but we ended up having some general conversation. Once I got to my stop, he gave me his number. We spoke briefly again, and I got off the train. I never called but saw him again when I visited a friend on the campus where he went to school. Nothing more came from those encounters, and I graduated a few months later.

School had ended, and my life at this point was calm. I was glad to be home with my family again, and I decided to enroll in graduate school to continue my education. For me, growing a relationship with God was what allowed me to have peace again, and life began to seem good. I felt like

I was headed in a good direction and was moving on from many of the heartaches and difficulties of my past.

One day, while out shopping, I ran into Otis again. I was shocked because I had never seen him in my area prior to now. My thoughts regarding him had not changed, and I felt no real interest still. Hence, our conversation was very short; and being that I was with other people, it made it easier to be brief. Upon ending the conversation, he gave me his number again, and I put it in my jacket pocket. I had no real intention to call, and it was several months before I decided to do so.

Looking back now, maybe there was a tugging in me not to be involved with Otis. I admit, there were no real sparks initially, and my focus and heart were elsewhere. So what made me finally call? Loneliness, familiarity, and seeking to one day have a family. Sometimes our decisions are not based on love but of convenience and fear. Without blame, sometimes we seek these relationships based on our own insecurities and past experiences. I can admit that this may have been my reasoning for going forward in what I knew was not what I truly desired.

So several months had passed, and I found Otis's number while cleaning out my jacket pocket. I figured there was no harm in calling, so I picked up the phone and dialed his number. Otis was shocked that I had even called, and surprisingly, the first conversation we had was a long one.

We talked about our brief encounters, about him, about me, about life, and about God.

Now, that was a biggie for me. My faith had grown since I attended college, and my main focus at this point was solely on God and his place in my life. We seemed to have a lot in common, and from what I could see, he appeared to be a "man of God." At the time, what that meant was that he knew the scriptures, could dialogue about them, and appeared to have a genuine desire to grow in his relationship with God. Now, I say *appeared* because I look back now and realize that knowing the scriptures is one thing, but having a true relationship with God is completely different. However, he seemed to be headed in the right direction.

Some time had passed, and we decided to go on a date. Our first date was dinner and out for a long drive. He was a gentleman the whole time, and we continued on this way for a while. Over time, I began to grow quite fond of him. As we progressed, I told him about the relationship that I had with Omar. I was adamant about not going through that experience again. I thought talking about it would let him know where my mind-set was and would prevent it from happening again. He appeared empathetic and concerned. However, I later realized that first impressions are just that, an impression. You have to really get to know people and then *pay attention* to the signals. I now realize that what I went through with Omar was a precursor for what I would go through with Otis.

How could you miss this again, Sasha? Well, as I mentioned earlier, loneliness, familiarity, and seeking to one day have a family was on the forefront of my mind. I just wasn't thinking as clearly as I should have. As a woman, you begin to hear the chatter of people about being married, having children, etc. And at this point—I was the ripe, old age of twenty-three—time was running out! At that time, I felt that I didn't want to miss another opportunity, and everyone talks about that "biological clock." The lies we tell ourselves can create the heartaches we later experience. The truth was that I had more than enough time to have a family. My heart was still elsewhere, and I just wanted what I thought I needed at the time. Wisdom in my later years gave me insight on the fact that I rushed to have what I still didn't get.

So as Otis and I continued on, things seemed "okay." However, over time, I began to see episodes of his mood shifts—from irritation to frustration and anger to rage. I justified not leaving him by saying, "Well, none of what he is doing has ever been directed toward me." I also thought that with me in the picture, Otis's life would improve and love would conquer all. "He just needs the right woman in his life," I told myself. I manipulated myself into being the person to make him happy, which was my fault. I became the one to think I could heal this broken vessel, and I became broken in the midst. So because I wanted what I wanted, I self-directed what could have been my own *total destruction*. Later, I learned that God's timing is the best timing.

After dating for about two years, he proposed to me, and I said yes. I was now going to be a "bride." Now, with planning a wedding, there was no turning back. Well, at least that was what I told myself. This process was an emotional roller coaster, and more of Otis's personality began to show. What I also didn't realize was that he had a history of mental-health concerns, which was more than I was prepared for.

When we were around each other, little things would turn into unnecessary arguments. Although part of me said this may not be the right path to take, I felt that I had invested so much into putting this wedding together that stopping it would cause both financial and emotional strain. From this experience, I learned that a marriage is not about the wedding but about the relationship. Getting so wrapped up in planning the wedding further made me ignore the emotional and mental pain that began to seep in. Instead of following my heart, I focused on not losing the money invested. However, doing that cost me a great deal more in both emotional and mental pain in the long run.

I remember the little arguments we had leading up to the big day. At times, we even argued on the way to our prewedding marriage counseling. That was a sign in and of itself. When we arrived to our sessions with the minister, we would act as if everything was *okay*. Looking back, I wish the pastor would have dug a little deeper during those sessions. Maybe things would have been different. I remember saying, "God, if he's not for me, please remove him from my path." In hindsight, I think he answered me, and I just went on with what I thought was right. The fact that I was going back and forth, contemplating, and didn't really feel settled about this decision was probably the answer to my prayer. I just didn't feel that I had the strength needed at the time to choose what I knew to be best for me.

So it was now the wedding day, and the final signs to call it off presented itself. There was a severe hurricane the day before, which shut down power across many areas. And on the day of the wedding, I hyperventilated in the limo on the way to the church as I wondered if I was doing the right thing or making the right decision. Part of my heart was still with Kendall; but by that time, I felt as if he had moved on, and so should I. Now, don't get me wrong. I did have love for Otis, but the relationship was not what I was seeking, and my heart knew it. But again, I wanted what I wanted, and thus I got what I got. But no one ever deserves the things that began to unfold when we finally said "I do."

Before I go to the next part of this journey, I would like to say something. If you don't have peace in a relationship, there is typically a reason for it. Maybe you are being triggered by your past, or maybe you're being triggered by something potentially not right as you move into your future. Listen to those thoughts and feelings and really look at why you may be feeling the way you do. For me, I looked at all the money spent for that wedding day and my loyalty to the situation. I also didn't want to hurt Otis by walking away when he had been there for me. All those illogical thoughts stopped my common sense. I knew where my heart was, and it wasn't with Otis truly. I made a decision based on comfort and convenience.

Reflection

After additional dating and then being engaged, things were revealed to me about Otis. He drank and smoked but hid that from me because he knew that I didn't like it. A potential mental-health disorder also existed but was undiagnosed. These things later added to the confusion and turmoil that emerged after we were married. If I had acted on what I knew and not on what I felt, it would have made a difference. Because of my desire to move in a direction that was not right for me, I added additional pain to myself.

No one deserves what came next, but I realized that not making good decisions in this situation put me on a path

I may have been able to avoid. We each have a role to play in these situations, and not walking away in the beginning before getting in too deep was the role I played. However, with that being said, still no one deserves to be abused, misused, or mistreated.

Otis

Honor Thy Husband

Soon after we were settled in as Mr. and Mrs., things continued on the path they were going. There were some good days, but a great deal of heartache came too. After we had been married for a few months, the arguing began to increase, and my emotional strength became shaky. I kept as hopeful as I could in order to combat some of the fiery darts thrown at me. I justified the mood swings as part of his mental-health symptoms, but that didn't relieve the stress that began to increase over time. I remember saying to him during an argument, "You are not my father, and you will *never* come before God in my life." To me, that was setting boundaries, stating what I wouldn't stand for; and for him, I think it was a challenge. Over time, he took that challenge to heart, and an increase of verbally abusive episodes began while the emotional abuse remained.

Almost two years after we were married, I found out that I was pregnant. He was excited initially and became the proud father-to-be. He was attentive toward me during the beginning of the pregnancy, but by the end, I guess the realization that the attention would change was more than he could bear. In the final stages, of the birth drawing near, he became somewhat irritated. The day that Sadie was born was supposed to be the happiest day for us, but like many days, it turned into more arguing and frustration. We made it through the birth, but after all of my family left, it was the worst experience a new mother could have. We argued about my family being in the delivery room, although previously he had agreed it was okay. He yelled and became more and more frustrated. All I could think was what it was going to be like when we arrived home.

Instead of staying at the hospital with me during this time, he left and went home. There was no support, no loving interactions, and none of the things I expected after just delivering the child we created together. After he left, with tears rolling down my cheek, I looked down at the blanket that held my precious daughter, Sadie. As I looked down at her, she looked back up at me with the brightest eyes. Crying in fear, loneliness, and pure frustration, I whispered, "It's going to be okay. God is going to take care of us, I promise."

Otis eventually came back to the hospital to pick us up and take us home. When we got there, the house was a mess. Now, prior to going to the hospital, I had cleaned during the nesting phase and expected to be able to come home and just rest. However, instead, I put my newborn to bed and went to cleaning. He helped and apologized for making the mess. After we were done, he went to get Sadie and sat with her; things were quiet for a bit. As I watched him interact with her, I prayed that things would stay just as they were at this moment. However, the moment was short-lived. In the days following, disconnect and additional strife was created each time attention was removed from him and placed on Sadie. Sadie spent most days with me, and although I was married, many times I felt like a single mom.

Over time, things *seemed* okay. However, walking on eggshells was the new mode of transportation in our home. It seemed like anything was a trigger, so I never knew when the tables would turn. There were arguments over and over again: the baby is crying, and he couldn't deal with it, or I was spending too much time doing things with the baby. After our child was born, things just seemed to have gone from bad to worse. Things still had not gotten physical at this point, but the verbal and emotional abuse was just as painful. Whoever said that "sticks and stones may break my bones, but words will never hurt me" lied. Words hurt worse because while you may be able to heal from the physical pain, the emotional pain has a lasting effect.

Over the years, things just seemed to get worse; and little by little, the testing of the physical abuse began. It started through retaliation on things that meant something to me, like breaking or throwing my angel figurines or other things that were given to me as gifts. He would, of course, apologize, typically after blaming me for getting him so upset in the first place. He would then say that he would never do it again, and then life was life again. The cycle of him being angry, making it my fault, apologizing, and then acting as if nothing ever happened just kept going. I continued to keep my head up, praying things would change. But they never really did.

During this time, the beginning of isolation started, and the mental abuse began to weigh me down. I felt myself becoming more and more confused. He would say things like, "Why are you spending so much time with your mom grocery shopping?" "Why aren't you spending that time with me?" Or I would explain something to him, and then he would reverse it to confuse what I said and make it as if I were saying something negative about him.

After some time, I was so confused that I began to say to myself, "Am I causing these outbursts?" The mental confusion, mixed with the ongoing fear and feelings of the daily need to walk on eggshells, was unbearable. I was filled with symptoms of depression and anxiety on a daily basis. However, when in public, I put on a good face, and no one was the wiser. Behind closed doors, I felt like I was a prisoner sentenced to life without the possibility of parole.

My life felt like a nightmare that I wish I could wake up from. Were there any good times, you ask? Well, yes there were, but the bad times outweighed them, and life just seemed like an ongoing whirlwind. Days free of arguing, fear, and frustrations were far and few. All I could do was pray things would get better one day, and that was what I held on to. In the meantime, I dealt with what I needed to and was thankful each day I made it through.

No one knew this secret journey, and I was too afraid to tell because of the shame, guilt, and fear. For goodness's sake, I have a graduate degree, good upbringing, and I'm smart—how did I let this happen? But again, we know that this situation is not based on any of that. At this point, I felt like I was in so deep that I couldn't get out, and I was also too afraid to reveal this on my own. I felt like a failure and just wanted someone to *find out* so this misery would stop.

Even with that being said, whether rational or not, I felt like he needed me, and the Bible says to work things out. I just wanted someone to find out so we could get help. Not being able to tell and feeling like I needed to stay attributed to me staying as long as I did. I also felt that our daughter needed to grow up in a household with both parents like I did. Otis didn't have that growing up. His father died in the war when he was younger, which may have breaded some anger. I wanted things to be different for our daughter. These were the irrational thoughts I told myself as I justified my inability to leave.

So now, in addition to finding my personal coping strategies, I now realized that I had to safeguard Sadie from the aftermath of the nonsense in this marriage. I knew there would be some effect, but I wanted to limit as much of the negativity as I could. I was still hopeful at this point that prayer could turn things around, and I tried to do all that I could. I didn't believe in divorce, and no one in my immediate family circle had ever been as far as I knew. "I chose this road, and I'm going to work this out," was what I told myself. What I also failed to tell myself was that God doesn't want his children to hurt. A husband is supposed to love you with unconditional love, and respect is supposed to go both ways.

You see, because Otis knew that I cherished my spiritual relationship, he would take scriptures and put his own spin on them. In my confusion, I even began to question my understanding of what I read. I had been so brainwashed that I wasn't sure if I was coming or going. And yet I couldn't find the courage to leave. In fact, part of me believed that I should still stay. Unless you have been in this situation, it seems hard to fathom. And it's these moments that change things from bad to even worse.

Reflection

Getting married does not stop the abuse you know is already there; it only makes it worse. As I look back, I see the continued signs that were evident from the start. My hope that things would change only added to the depth of where I eventually headed. I now felt trapped and on top of it; I had brought another life into this chaos. At this point, I felt that my life was spinning out of control. Why was this happening to me? What did I do to deserve this? I always imagined being able to enjoy a wonderful life with a loving husband, a few wonderful children, and a great career. This was not the case, and I could not understand where I went wrong. This just did not make sense and, like many, I felt stuck.

Over time, I realized that the length of time spent in these relationships affects the ability to leave. When a child is added to the mix, the difficulty becomes even greater. In some cases, the abuser may use the child as an additional punishment or pawn. They may threaten to harm the child should attempts be made to leave them, or they may attempt to turn the child against you. There is now a felt obligation to stay although the desire is to leave. The ongoing agony increases depression, lowers self-esteem even further, and increases silence for the victim. For all these reasons and more, many feel led to stay in these relationships although unhealthy.

Otis

When Will It End

As our child got older, we brought our first home so that we had more indoor and outdoor space for Sadie to play. This was when the full physical abuse began. It seemed like the more I spent time with our child, the worse it got. He hated it and appeared jealous. He began to get upset that I spent time with anyone but him, including our child. Doing her hair took too long, me shopping with my mom or siblings took too long, everything that didn't center on him was too long. This became very evident when we were invited to my cousin's wedding.

I remember discussing with Otis that I wanted to attend because the wedding was for a close relative, and it was also around the day of my birthday. So for me, it was celebrating their wedding and my birthday. To my surprise, Otis agreed to go. We had a sitter and everything. Things were in place, and I felt like this would be a nice experience for us. Up until now, we never went to anything together or went out for that matter. However, it was short-lived; and at the last minute, he decided that he wasn't going. And to top it off, because he had chosen not to attend, he expected me to stay home as well. When I expressed that I wouldn't, he made it appear as if he was okay with me going. However, unbeknownst to me, while I went to the wedding, he sat and stewed.

The wedding was wonderful, and now it was time for me to return home. When I returned home, there was a panic as I realized I had arrived a little later than I expected. As I turned the key to the front door, all the fun I felt from being out and enjoying myself immediately dropped, and I felt sick. When I walked in the door, Otis was sitting on the couch with a smile on his face. I walked in and said, "Hi, Otis," thinking that, just maybe, things would be okay. He responded pleasantly and asked about my night (e.g., how the wedding was, what I did, what I ate, and who I was with). He appeared interested in the evening, and his tone wasn't an angry one, so I felt as if things would be okay. When the conversation was done, things were still peaceful, so I got up to shower and change my clothing. When I returned to the living room, he was still sitting on the couch. However, like Dr. Jekyll and Mr. Hyde, his mood had shifted; and he now sat with a psychotic look in his eyes, holding a long stick. He had screwed the plastic handle from the mop and stared me down, as he stomped the stick on the floor.

Everything in me just wanted to die because I didn't know what was about to happen. The argument started, and the fear rose in me. As he hovered over me, he grabbed, pushed, shoved, and belittled me—all I could think of was Sadie, who was asleep in the next room. Why was this happening? I wanted it to just stop. He continued to grab and shove me while insulting me and accusing me of being with someone else, neglecting our child because I went out, and not being a good wife. I was being punished for spending time with family and not choosing to stay home with him.

The fear continued to increase as I waited to see what he would do with the stick. He, however, never hit me with it but used it to continually intimidate me as if he would use it. After he was done with me, I was finally allowed to see my daughter and go to bed. Later that night, after the storm subsided, his desire to be intimate emerged. Conflicted in thoughts, I obliged in order to maintain some level of peace.

Over time, this cycle of events continued. I became depressed, and subtle changes became more evident. People I worked with began to notice that I was changing; I looked different, and my mood was always off. Yet as much as I wanted to admit what was happening, I could not. I was fearful of what Otis would do if anyone found out. I was also fearful of how others would look at me because I was staying, and irrationally, I was fearful that I was ruining the family I was trying to create. In not being able to tell, I became good at making excuses about what I was going through (e.g., burnout, overtired, overwhelmed, etc). I also learned how to mask my emotions so that people wouldn't ask me what was wrong. This took a lot of energy to do each week, but it was something I felt I needed to do.

The longer I stayed, the more intense things got, especially during the weekends. On the weekends, I just wanted to relax, but that was not an option. I began to hate Fridays, Saturdays, and Sundays. These were the days that I had no escape or break from being around him. On Fridays, I would prepare myself because I never knew how much agony I would go through between then and Monday. Wanting to relax was a huge argument. How dare I want to relax and not spend every waking moment with him? I worked all week, and the weekend was to be "family time." This really meant Otis time.

Trying to find ways to have peace, I bought him a gym membership. That didn't last long. Instead of him going during the afternoon or evening, he just went while Sadie and I were asleep so that we could spend "family time together" during the day. Frustrated and depressed, the weekends were not very enjoyable and filled with ongoing arguments that led to being pushed, shoved, hit, belittled, insulted, yelled at, and just depleted. Running out of options, I finally confided in a few people. I felt a continued death each day that passed and needed help. I, however, knew that although it was bad, I wasn't prepared to leave yet. Part of this feeling stemmed from being afraid that I would shame my family if this came out.

The individuals whom I spoke to were very supportive. They listened to me, and I finally felt like maybe, just maybe, something could be done. But because of my fear, I didn't want them to do too much. I especially did not want them to call the police. Irrational, yes that was. But at the time, the fear overshadowed thinking clearly. I just felt that getting the police involved would make my life worse. I know much different now and wish I had called. I look back and realize that although I told someone, I was still too afraid for any true intervention. I also minimized what I told them so that it didn't seem so bad. All these things hindered me from getting the help I truly needed.

Confidentially, I also spoke to my pastor, thinking that he could do more. My demeanor and physical appearance had dramatically changed over the years, so I felt that he would say, "I was waiting for you to reveal this so I could help." But that was not the case. Although I minimized some aspects of what I experienced, I felt that if anyone could help me, my pastor could. When I spoke to him, I subtly let him know that things were "not okay" in my house. He asked about the physical abuse, but of course, with the shame I felt, I downplayed it. I'm not sure what I expected, but I didn't feel like I was supported as much as I needed. The pastor pretty much expressed that this was more spiritual than not. Now at this point, I had already rationalized that what I was going through maybe spiritual. However, with all that had been going on, I knew that just being a spiritual issue was not the whole answer. Needless to say, having him further emphasize the spiritual aspect was not what I really needed at that time. It just further minimized what was truly happening.

Although I wasn't making that much headway, I continued to have meetings with my pastor periodically. Sometimes I felt relieved because I was gaining some strength and support. However, to some degree, I felt worse. I needed more than just prayer and discussion regarding my husband needing to come to church. By this point, I wanted my husband to be confronted and stopped.

So the agony continued, and there was no real resolve. I felt like the fear overpowered me so much so that even with the support I had, I felt like there was none. I no longer knew what to do. What I truly wanted was for someone to just call the police during one of our loud arguments and pull me out of the situation. I felt like I would never get out and would just be stuck. So I went into survival mode, not knowing what else to do. Within the four years of marriage, I had gone from a lively and vibrant woman to a timid and depressed woman with suicidal thoughts.

In my earlier recalls, I did not provide you with specific incidents. However, I would like to do so now so that you can get a picture of what causes the paralyzed fear that confuses a person to stay. Over the span of the marriage, there were so many incidents that I would not be able to retell them all. However, I wanted to share some of my journal entries with you to help you further understand the nature of what I endured for so many years. The following are excerpts from my journal entries:

Dear diary,

Today I took Sadie to the doctor. During her exam, the doctor used me to show her how she would look into her ears with the otoscope. When her doctor looked into my ears, she noticed that my eardrum had burst. When she asked how it happened, I couldn't bear to tell her the truth that Otis and I got into an argument two days prior and that, during the argument, he was angry yet again and hit me across the head. I remember hearing my ear pop right before I briefly blacked out. So instead, as usual, I made an excuse so that my little secret didn't get out. I don't think the doctor fully believed me, but there was nothing else she could do. Deep down, I wish something was revealed so that someone could finally help me because, Lord, I don't have the strength.

Dear diary,

Today I cooked a good meal—fried chicken, rice, and vegetables. Sadie was hungry, and so I fed her first. And while doing so, I took a little slither of chicken for myself. Well, in doing that, it set Otis off. He began to yell and cuss at me, calling me a dumb b——, stupid, and a bunch of other names. How dare I eat before he does and not wait to eat together as a family? So instead of realizing that it was not a whole meal and that it was just a slither of chicken, he decided that no one was going to eat and took everything that I had cooked and threw it into the garbage…

Dear diary,

Today I can sadly say that I have some inkling as to what it feels like to be raped. Yesterday I had been sick all day and still sick today. My temperature yesterday was 102. I was hot to the touch, stomach aching, throwing up during the day, and just not feeling well overall. With all of that, I still managed to take care of Sadie for the better part of the day.

Well, I guess because I took care of Sadie, Otis felt that I could take care of him too. As I lay down to rest and tried to break this fever, I began to feel Otis lie next to me. I thought he was trying to comfort me, but he had other things on his mind.

As I lay there trying to rest, I began to feel him kissing on me. "Stop," I said in a groggy voice. But he continued rubbing on me and kissing me. "Stop. I don't feel good." Nothing I said was making him stop. Irritated and weakened, I tried to push him away from me, but he just kept trying to talk me into just relaxing as he continued what he was doing. With little energy, I just lay there as he pleasured himself. I just kept saying to myself, *God make this stop. Let it be over.* Thoughts ran through my mind: *I now know some of what it feels like to be raped.*

It's one thing for me to just not be in the mood but perform my wifely duties anyway. It's another thing to have a fever, not feel well, and be forced without regard. I felt dirty and even sicker. I was disgusted by his lack of regard toward me, and my discontent for him is growing even more.

Dear diary,

God, when will this end? Today I'm getting lower and lower in my faith, in my mind, and weakened in my body. Today Otis and I were arguing about work schedules, food and something else. I told him that I didn't have time for this, that I needed to get ready for work. He continued to get in my face, intimidating me with his body and yelling. I just turned and walked toward the bathroom so I could take my shower. I could hear him still yelling as I stepped into the tub. When I turned around, he was in the bathroom, closing the door behind him.

I could hear Sadie screaming and crying for me on the other side of the door. I tried to leave to get to her, and he threw me up against the shower wall. I pleaded for him to stop, but he just grabbed my arms and tossed me around the shower walls. I yelled and screamed for him to stop as I continued to hear Sadie outside the door. Just then, as I thought he was leaving, he turned around, grabbed the handheld showerhead, and threw it in my direction, hitting both me and the wall. He then finally left the bathroom and picked up Sadie.

Lord, I know you saw me as I just sobbed and called out to you. God, when will this end? I'm look-

ing at my arms now, and I have bruises on them.
When I went into the room, I just sat in the corner,
and Sadie came over to me as usual to console me.
Lord, I can't put her through this anymore. Give me
the strength to do something. Please, Lord, please!

There were many more incidents, but as I said earlier,
there are too many to mention. Those were just some of
the things that I had to endure. Day-to-day life had its ups
and downs, and most of the time, I walked on eggshells.
I remember, as time went on, Otis frequently having the
stick he walked around the house with. It was the handle of the broom that he had twisted off. When the stick
came out, that meant he was upset and things were going
to become difficult. Many times he would pull out the stick
just to intimidate me. He would challenge me to give him a
reason to attempt to use it, but ultimately never hit me with
it. I lived like this for a while; and no matter how much I
prayed, I felt lost, hopeless, and helpless.

After enduring this for almost four years, I slipped into
a deep depression and lost over forty pounds. I remember
just wanting to die as I reexamined my life. I thought, *Is this
it? Is this how my life is going to be?* I was somewhat isolated
and just felt stuck. I didn't want to stay and didn't have the
strength to go. I was also distressed in thinking about how
Sadie always came over to console me after the incidents.

What was this doing to her? What was this teaching her? I was dying inside but began to think, *What would it do to our family or me if I called the police?* I lived in constant fear and misery. Until one day, I got an open door.

This is my journal entry when the door finally seemed to open:

Dear diary,

Yesterday there was so much that went on that I just don't know anymore. Otis came home from work upset. He had been at work and called me repeatedly to argue with me about not paying much attention to him before he went to work. When he got home, he began drinking and smoking and started arguing with me again. I had had enough and picked up Sadie, who at this point was crying. As I was holding her, he started throwing bags of laundry at me while calling me names. He began to become very intimidating, and as I attempted to leave, he tried to block me. He was irate, and I was fearful, not knowing what he was going to do next. I was afraid for me and the safety of my Sadie.

I was finally able to make it out of the house and to my car as he threatened me not to go to my parents. I drove around for an hour and finally parked in the parking lot of a movie theater. I sat there, too afraid to go to my parents and too afraid to go back home. He called me repeatedly, yelling and threatening to hurt me if I went to my parents. I had never gotten to the point of being this scared. My fear level had increased so much that I didn't know what to do. But I knew I couldn't go back. No one really knew about our relationship, and at that point, I just felt alone in my pain.

I finally got up the courage to call my close friend Yazmine so that I could calm myself down until I figured out what I should do. We talked for almost two hours while my husband kept attempting to call me on the other line. After talking with Yazmine, she convinced me to come to her home for the night. When I got there, my parents met me at the door. I looked at them with a petrified look on my face, not in fear but in shame. I then began to sob while holding my daughter. My parents came over to me and put their arms around me. I felt such a weight lift off me. The secret was not a secret anymore. I had been waiting for this moment and thought it would never come.

Otis continued to call me, and my parents answered the phone. I was fearful as to what he would do because he specifically told me not to go to my parents. But I was glad that they finally knew.

There was a level of relief that this was no longer a secret. I stayed with my parents overnight, but I didn't know what my next move would be. We will see what happens next.

Reflection

Reflecting on these moments was very difficult for me. What do I say? As I look back on my experiences, all I see is fear—paralyzing fear. The day I left the house was a day I remember just feeling terrified. There was no end in sight. How did I live through this day in and day out? The torment, the hurt, pain, and ultimate loss of myself; I was slowly dwindling away! The distress, frustration, and depression overshadowed the hope, dreams, and desires I once had. If it had not been for my friend, I'm not sure what would have happened. This was a turning point in my life.

I've asked myself, *What would have happened if my parents were never called and intervened?* All I can do is fathom what the outcome would have been. I am blessed that my friend reached out when I couldn't because that night I was truly in fear for my life and that of my child. Support is the most important resource for someone going through this experience. You never know when that one moment of reaching out may be the turning point in someone's life.

Otis

Crying Out

It has now been five years, and during this time, things have gotten worse, even though my parents now know. Things got better for a moment but returned to the cycle it once was. I began to become stronger and feel weaker all at the same time. I was stuck again in my situation, continually depressed and losing weight. I felt like I was slowly dying a painful death with no real hope in sight. The torment increased, and my mind just began to let go. I couldn't make sense of anything, and I just wanted to disconnect from it all. I wished I had a time machine that could turn back the hands of time, but I didn't. I felt alone, hurt, and ashamed. And although I still sought direction from God, I felt disregarded and questioned if I was being punished for making the decision to marry Otis.

I remember late one night saying to myself, *I give up. I can't take this anymore!* I went to the little nook in the hallway, which I made into my prayer corner, and just began to sob softly. I began to pray and rattle off my thoughts to God. *Why am I going through all of this? What did I do to deserve this? How did I let this happen again? I told Otis about what had happened to me previously, and he made it a hundred times worse. Why did I say yes? This torment is unbearable. Will it ever end? I don't see a way out.* At this time, I just felt hopeless and helpless, and I just wanted to die so this can all be over. "I just want to die"—I kept saying over and over again. *God, I've never hated anyone in my life, but forgive me because I truly hate Otis for what he has and continues to do to me.*

Just then, I thought about Sadie. If I died, I would be leaving her with him, and what would her life be? I couldn't let that happen. I had to fight and pray for something to change. This was what I kept telling myself. As I kneeled down on the soft carpet, the tears continued to stream down my face. Just then, I remembered a gospel song I had heard the other day called "You Survived" (by James Fortune and Fiya). I then said, "Lord, HELP ME! This is hard for me! My life has not gone quite the way I had planned it. All I asked for was a good marriage, a few kids, and a productive career. Was that too much to ask for? LORD! I feel lost. I don't know where my life is going from here. I am hurting, and I don't know what to do anymore. Lord, O Lord! What is next for me?" I continued to open my heart and cried and cried as the tears continued to stream down my cheeks. I eventually calmed down and went to lay on the couch until I fell asleep.

The next night, I went through the same thing again and just needed answers. I began to write in my journal:

Dear diary,

Lord, it's been five years, and here we go again. I left shortly once and thought we could work this out, but it's just getting worse. Lord, I can't take this anymore. What did I do to deserve this life? I have done all that I know how to do. I've been a submissive wife, doing all that it entails. I pray to you. I hold my tongue, even though he is the way he is. I show respect (although I know he would beg to differ). Yet nothing changes. Tearfully I yell out to you, "LORD I'M CRYING OUT TO YOU! HELP ME SEE MY WAY CLEAR—HELP ME TO UNDERSTAND WHY I AM SUFFERING!" I am a good wife and mother. What does he want from me! My heart is hurting, and I don't know what to do anymore.

As I wrote, tears continued to stream down my face. I then began to whisper to myself as if I were in excruciating pain, "Lord, I want to take my life right now. I don't want to do this anymore." I didn't know how I would do it, but I just wanted to die. And again, I began to think of my daughter, Sadie. What will her life be with me gone?

The following night, I watched TBN (Trinity Broadcasting Network) and saw the story of Joseph. I never sat to watch these stories, but that night I did. I related to him: the persecution, the imprisonment, and the vision that finally came to pass. It had given me additional hope to continue. Over the next few days, my mind-set changed, and I saw myself in a different light. I began to reread some of my journal entries, and one in particular made me mad. It was a letter that I wrote to my husband, which I never gave him. I never truly felt like I could talk to him, so from time to time, I would write a letter as if I could. This is what the letter said:

Letter to Otis

July 23, 2012

Dear Otis,

Why are you always so upset with me? I feel like I can't truly be myself because you seem to be annoyed with so many things that I do. When you get upset with me, you hold a grudge instead of just speaking to me, and this is very emotionally draining, trying to figure out what I did wrong. Your mood changes then you get up, go smoke, and drink. This is a pattern you have with me, and I don't know why. There are times you tell me I'm not speaking to you; but I don't find that out until I ask you because instead of you telling me, you just get upset and mope around the house, mad.

Last night, you got mad at me for not doing anything. I'm not sure what you wanted me to do. You were tired most of the night. You took a shower. I asked you if you felt better, and you said yes. You lay down and was dozing off, so I left you alone—meaning, I stayed quiet so you could rest. We talked about the poker thing for a little while then watched the football game. What did I do wrong? What did you want me to do? Instead of getting so mad at me, can you talk to me instead? I'm writing you because I feel I can express myself a little better this way.

Sometimes when I talk to you, my words get muddled and I feel like you are waiting to catch me saying something wrong so you can use it against me, and because of that, sometimes my words get jumbled. I want to know from you why I annoy you so much to the point that you hold grudges against me. You shut down without me even knowing what I did to make you upset. I'm tired of being emotionally drained because of this. Most of the time, when you are upset with me, it's not stuff that I feel are that serious to be mad about. If you feel different, let me know; but to me, some of this stuff is not worth the tension it causes. I feel like if something should happen to us (God forbid), I don't want things like this to be the last we remember of each other. I feel like so much energy is given to these issues where they can be taken care of when they occur. I love you, but I don't know what to do to stop feeling like this and causing you constant annoyance.

Don't get me wrong. We do have times where things are really good, and we seem very happy, and I feel okay. It's just in the times I mentioned above where I need clarity. I feel confused and don't know how to respond in those situations because I'm beginning to feel numb—meaning that when you get mad at me and hold grudges and I don't know what I did wrong, I don't want to feel anymore. I don't know what I did. I don't know what to say. I feel I'll annoy you more by saying something; but I don't want to feel that way or prolong the situation, so I attempt to say something, which at times annoys you even more, which I don't mean to do. There are times I don't say anything until you say something so that I know when you are mad at me. I just don't know why most times. I just want peace in my life and not all the tension and turmoil. Please help me understand why you get so upset with me so that I can try to make changes. I love you, and I don't want to continue to cause you pain from things I may do. I don't know what else to say. I want things to get better, and I hope this helps.

Love,
Sasha

As I reread this letter, I realized how jumbled my thoughts had been. The fear of saying the wrong words and the confusion was evident even in the letter. It sickened me to read how apologetic I was. I was the one who had taken the brunt of his reactive behaviors, and I'm apologizing. The apologizing out of fear was an ongoing thing, and I started to see this relationship for what it was. I had finally hit my rock bottom. No more. I deserve better than this! I was tired of the nonsense, and I started to gain new strength. I also began to realize that my daughter was seeing all of this. What will that do to her? She had already had a behavioral episode in school in which she became enraged with another student and grabbed her by the hair. I began to think, *What else am I teaching her by staying?*

The next day, I just needed to get away and find the answers that I was searching for. I went to church but didn't want to talk to anyone inside. Instead, I just sat in the church parking lot. There was no one but me; and I cried, prayed, and just asked why. I then called Nicole, in whom

I had confided some information, and just cried out to her. She talked to me, comforted me, and then said, "You have said you would leave but haven't done so yet. If God said leave, will you leave?"

I had finally hit my rock bottom. I had had enough. I was at the end of my rope. I had lost over forty pounds since marriage. I hated the weekends. I hated my life, and I hated him! I had never had so much hatred in my heart. So what was your answer, Sasha, you ask? It was *yes*! "I can't do this anymore," I cried. She then prayed with me for strength and an open door.

Reflection

Rock bottom finally reached. However, even at this point—without support or a clear plan and direction—the constant state of confusion was ongoing. I felt stuck yet again. Things get better and then, like clockwork, get worse. This cycle goes on and on with no end in sight. One minute things are okay, given the false hope that a change may still be possible. However, not far behind is the tension that starts—typically for no reason and then said to be your fault. So now you're the reason for the anger and begin to apologize because you know where this leads. And before you know it, hands, fist, and objects start flying. Once it's all done, you hear, "I don't want to hurt you, but you just make me so mad. You know what I'm going through. Why can't you just stop making me upset?" You now feel guilty, and making up comes shortly thereafter (cuddling, hugging, kissing, etc). For the next few minutes, hours, or days, things seem okay, until it starts all over again. Sound familiar?

Going through this over and over again increases the feeling of being stuck. You want to go but can't because of fear, confusion, and low self-esteem. And to some degree, depending on the level of danger or threat, you may have to stay until able to leave. Without a support system or planning, leaving is not a reality. Never knowing when this will end and feeling fearful of how it will end become a daily reminder of your lack of control over your life. This is the ongoing mind-set of being in this situation and another reason why many find it so difficult to leave.

Otis

The Day We Parted Ways

I was at the end and had no more strength. After that prayer and conversation, I felt a sense of peace. Things after that moment seemed to just fall into place. Within a week of that conversation, the door flew open for me, and the opportunity presented itself for me to finally stand up for myself. I began to see things clearer and wanted my life back. I started feeling like I could leave, and it was different from the past where I would say, "If he does this one more time, I'm leaving," but then still stayed.

So the days went by, and I began my strategy for leaving. I had my shoes, keys, and purse by the door and just felt like one more time, and I was leaving. I didn't have to worry about finances because I had my own and I had a place to stay at my parents'. Things were in place, and I was ready. So the week started, and he was already angry: I spent too much time doing our daughter's hair. Then my father stopped by to visit and check on me, which just made Otis more irritated. The ball was rolling, and the day finally came. Now, why didn't I just leave? Well, I had some strength, but the fear still stopped me from just leaving. I felt that I needed an in-the-moment reason to leave. Now, keep in mind that I knew the level of threat and felt I could handle it. If there was a higher threat level, I probably would have made myself leave before then.

I knew time was getting close for leaving when I was reminded of the phone call I received from Sadie's preschool, saying that she became angry with another child who took something from her. The teacher began to say that Sadie grabbed the other child by the hair with such anger that she pulled out some of the child's hair. At that point, I knew that I was definitely not shielding her from all that I thought I was. She was picking up on everything she heard and the things I didn't think she saw. It was a revelation moment, and I knew it was just a matter of time before I would leave Otis.

So my day of independence was in early November, which is typically cold. However, on this day, it was one of the warmest and sunniest days. The week itself had felt peaceful, although there had been a buildup of little things that would contribute to the weekend arguing time. The events of the day unfolded, and I was as prepared as I could be. I remember that on that day I was cleaning Sadie's room. Just then, I heard Otis mumbling and the stick clacking on the floor. My anxiety went up, but I knew this was it and that it was just a matter of time.

Otis came in the room with the "fear stick" and began fussing at me. I was surprisingly calm and responded in a way that he was not typically used to, which just enraged him even more. I looked toward Sadie, who was in front of me, and strategized what I would need to do in any given situation. I then looked at him out of the corner of my eye as he paced back and forth with continued mumbling. Confused and fed up, he approached me, saying, "I can't stand you. You make me sick. You disgust me. Tomorrow I'm going down to the courthouse, and I'm filing for a divorce. I can't do this anymore."

Just at that moment, this scripture came to my mind: "It has been said, 'Anyone who divorces his wife must give her a certificate of divorce'" (Matt. 5:31). In my mind, it was time. So my response to him was, "Good. I was thinking the same thing." That statement sent everything into full throttle. He was truly infuriated now. I had never responded in that fashion. Typically I would say, "Stop saying things like that before it happens." This time, I was officially done. As strong as I felt, I was also as weak and scared. But peace continued to keep me calm, and I knew this would soon be over one way or another.

With my statement, he paced more, and his face looked as if the devil himself had come out. He began to swing the stick around and accidently hit Sadie on her foot. That was the extra strength that I needed to say, "NO MORE!" I picked up Sadie and was able to safely make it toward the kitchen to the back door. He then took Sadie out of my arms because he knew I would never leave without her. He held her hostage in a sense. I prayed to myself, *Lord, help me.*

Panic started in my mind while I tried to figure out how to get Sadie and leave. Otis, at this time, had chased me back into the kitchen. He stood in front of me, close enough for me to feel his breath and heartbeat mixed with my fear and desire to fight back. He then put Sadie down, and I watched her walk back and forth in the living room, crying at the top of her lungs. While he stood blocking the entrance to the living room, I envisioned in my mind where my shoes were, where the keys were, and where Sadie was.

Each time Sadie attempted to come near me, Otis moved her back into the living room. I watched as tears streamed down her face, with a hyperventilating scream at the top of her lungs. The worst feeling for a mother is to see her child hurt in any way. *Do what you will to me*, I said to myself, *but you will NOT hurt her*.

I dashed to try again to get her, and he blocked me. I managed to get the phone and tried dialing my parents in secret. However, he came into the kitchen just as my parents' answering machine came on, so I hung up. *Lord, help me!* I kept saying to myself. As Otis paced back and forth in rage, I received my opening to grab Sadie. I finally had her in my arms and was not letting her go. As he paced back and forth in and out of the kitchen, I was able to put on my shoes. Just then, I heard Sadie, who was now about three, say in a tearful voice, "Mommy, I want to leave." That was all I needed to confirm that it was time.

I made an attempt toward my keys and pocketbook, but he stood in front of Sadie and me, yelling and cussing. With a quickness of his hand, he grabbed me by the neck. His muscular, abrasive fingers wrapped themselves around my neck, and he lifted me onto the counter while I still had Sadie in my arms. All I could hear was Sadie crying and my will to leave. I later saw that I had a skin burn on my neck from the amount of pressure he had applied to my neck. Thank God that he did not crush my throat.

With tears beginning to stream down my face and his inaudible voice blaring, he finally let go and walked to the living room, where he began to pace again. I then jumped down off the counter where he had lifted and seated me and made a dash for my pocketbook and keys. Sadie and I then headed toward the door and made a beeline for the car sitting in our parking area. I hurriedly placed Sadie in her car seat with trembling hands and walked toward the driver's door. I quickly took note of the weather and realized that Sadie had only shorts and a short-sleeved shirt on with no shoes on her feet. I had on shorts, sandals, and a short-sleeved shirt. Now, this was the middle of November and an unordinary day. This continued to confirm that it was definitely my time to leave. Everything fell into place.

As I began to drive off, he screamed, "Where are you going?" I yelled back, "I am done, and I'm not doing this anymore. I'm leaving you." I then began to peel out of the parking lot. He attempted to jump in front of the car until he realized that I wasn't stopping, and he quickly moved. I drove directly to my parents' home. He continued to call me my whole ride there, and I continued not to answer. When I arrived at my parents' home, they had just arrived from running errands for the day. With tears streaming down my face, I said, "I'm done. It's over." I remember my father embracing me and saying, "I knew you would come home when you were ready." It was like God opening his arms to me, saying, "It's over now. I got you." That was the day the healing began.

On that unusual November day, doors closed, and new ones opened. After almost six years, I had finally left, and I did not turn back. I had the strength to leave, but the next steps were not so easy. I am thankful that I have a very supportive and loving family because without them, I'm not sure I would have made it through. Although I had left Otis physically—emotionally and mentally, I was still there. My belief in marriage and sticking by my spouse tormented me as I began to see my future as bleak. This was such an untruth, but I had been through so much that I felt like recovering would be something that was so far away. I didn't believe in divorce, but here I was, in the process of it and now a single mother. This was never the life I saw for myself, and I didn't know how I got to this point.

Reflections

I'm not sure I ever saw this day coming, but it finally did. Almost Six years had passed, and I just hoped things would change. What I finally realized was that it was me who had to change. I had to get fed up with the life I was living. I had to desire more for my life and for my daughter. Through God, family, and friends, I was able to see that things were never going to change and that it was over. What a relief, right? Well, now I was about to be divorced and a single mom. One challenge ended, and new ones came.

Although it was not what I intended for my life, I made it, and I learned from it. And what I have learned, I can now share with you. Many times I felt alone, abandoned, and overlooked, thinking that God had forgotten me. But over time, I realized that he never did. How can I say that after all I endured? I can say that because I am here and able to share my journey with you. Like Joseph in the Bible, I went through unfair trials while waiting on God. But through it all, even when I didn't see happiness or a true end, I never stopped praying, believing, and fighting for something better.

I say all this to remind you to hang in there. You are not alone, even when you feel like it. I know that it is hard and, at times, easier said than done but find your inner strength. Like a boxer in the last round who feels like just giving up, take a deep breath and stay in the ring. I know that everyone's journey is different, but if you are able to gain that additional strength, it may help to get you to a better place. Always remember safety first, and having support helps tremendously. This is not a fight you can do on your own.

3

Divorce
There Is Purpose in Your Pain

Otis

Closed Doors Bring Opened Doors

DAYS WENT BY, and the reality had not quite set in for Otis. We were separated, but he still felt like I would come back like I had before. It was rough for him, so it appeared, as it was for me. Our separation came right before Thanksgiving, and for the first time, I saw him have a meltdown. He pleaded for another chance and tried to encourage me to come back. He claimed that he would "never lay hands on me again." As heartwarming as that was, I was now aware of the cycle. I knew that it would be short-lived and that it was just a matter of time before the angry Otis would resurface.

After my continued resistance to his desires to "rekin-dle" what we had, the old Otis did return. Like Dr. Jekyll and Mr. Hyde, one minute he was loving toward me; and the next minute, he was enraged and furious. And yet again, it was, of course, my fault. I caused the issues because I left, because I wouldn't try, because I was a so and so, and ulti-mately, because he never took responsibility for his actions.

So there we were, separated, and I was seeking to even-tually proceed with divorce. Separation and divorce is a process in and of itself. Add in abuse, and that becomes an even longer process. The torment didn't stop just because we weren't together. He just found new ways to do it from afar. So instead of hitting me, he carried on the fear by tormenting me through repeated phone calls, every day and every night. He not only called me, but he called my parents' home phone as well. This was nonstop torment, and I didn't know how not to respond to it. The fear still remained even though the immediate danger had lifted.

My family attempted to convince me not to answer the phone calls, but it seemed as if it just got worse when I didn't. Will this ever end? So you could have called the police, Sasha. Well, again, not that easy. When your mind-set is based on fear, you don't think "rationally." You think out of fear. What will happen if I do this, and what will hap-pen if I do that? Whether the danger is there truly or you think it will be is why the response remains the same. This, in and of itself, represents symptoms of PTSD, in which a person is triggered to think that they will be harmed even when they may not be in immediate or imminent danger at that moment.

After some time had passed, I grew stronger. Having a good support system is very important to healing and gaining the strength needed to move on. My family comforted me and showed their ongoing love toward me. They assisted me through the depressed times, the fearful times, and the emotional times. It was nourishment that helped me both mentally and physically. Over time, I increased in weight, my mood was happier, and I felt a sense of peace. As I continued to get stronger in all those areas, I also regained my strength spiritually.

In finding peace again, I realized how bitter and angry I was. I was mad about so much and mad at so many, including myself. Thoughts that I began to have were, *Why didn't I stop when I saw the red flags? Why did I go on knowing in my heart that he was not the right road for me to travel? Everyone saw the changes in my mood, my attitude, and my appearance— that was my cry for help. Where was everyone?* I needed them. Maybe they didn't know what to do or how to handle this.

I was mad at my pastor for not doing more. I was mad at my family for not saying something is not right and investigating. I was mad at God for allowing me to go through this and waste my time, making me feel as though I lost my future dreams of not having another child, not knowing what to do next, and being wounded. Most of all, I was mad at me for not saying, "No, I'm not going to marry you," and giving the ring back in the beginning. These were my feelings as I processed through my pain. I felt so alone, confused, hurt, and depleted. Here I was, this strong-willed, strong-minded person; and through this part of the journey, I was beaten down and knocked around.

Once I got to a place where I could let go of the bitterness that I felt, I began to feel sorry for Otis. I began to feel sorry that he felt the need to gain love in such an intrusive and violent way. I felt sorry that he didn't truly know how to love and receive love that was unconditional. I felt sorry that he didn't bother to look at what he was doing to us, our daughter, our marriage, or himself. And I truly felt sorry that his life had hurt him so much, that he felt the need to hurt others in return.

How can you feel bad for him, Sasha? Well, in order for me to heal, I had to let go of his hold on me. And to do that, I had to forgive him. The forgiveness was to release me from the bondage of the pain of my past. It was hard, let me tell you—not easy at all since he continued to call repeatedly and torment me. But I had to get to a place in my heart that would prevent me from turning cold and loving in the manner that he did. As the quote says, "Hurt people hurt people." I did not want to be that person who hurts someone else. I want to continue to be able to love and love unconditionally. I forgave him for feeling the need to hurt me—but not in a way that condones what he did or, in a way, to say, "I accept you back into my life." That is not the case. Through my forgiveness, I learned to move on, create boundaries, and reshape the interactions that we have, if any. Forgiveness was what I had to do to understand and give meaning to what I had to endure.

So a few months passed. It took some time for me to follow through with the divorce process. Emotionally and financially, I had to prepare myself. I felt as though it would be another torment in my life and that it would create additional issues. But through prayer and faith, it was a smooth transition. No contesting, no arguing, and no staying in the way of the process. Although Otis never apologized or admitted to his actions, I took this as a peace offering. So after almost a year, we were finally divorced, and I began to feel free.

Now, although the divorce was final, the behaviors didn't subside for a while. He continued to express desire to get back together, to act as if we could be friends, or to attempt being supportive toward me. However, with the cycle of abuse, I created boundaries so that I would not go backward. With this door now closed, I began looking at the new doors opened in front of me. It was now time to reinvent myself. But in order to do that, I had to also realize that I had to help Sadie get through the emotional pain placed on her by this ordeal. I wasn't the only one who lost something. Sadie lost as well, and it was going to be a process to rebuild her trust, emotional stability, and anything else that she may have been going through as a result.

Reflection

It is because of this experience that I don't want anyone else to suffer in silence. I wanted others to do for me what I could not and would not do for myself. Although no one knew the extent of my suffering, I was screaming out. No one heard me, or they heard me and didn't know what to do. I want you to know what to do. Lives may be saved by not ignoring it.

As you can see, I went back and forth many times. However, prayer and knowing I had support gave me the strength I needed to move forward. Support is needed in order to stay free and continue to focus on improvement. Just because a person has gained the ability to leave does not mean it is over. To be honest, it's just the beginning for all parties involved.

Living through this typically results in some form of PTSD, and depression continues to be a struggle. However, recreating the self, building self-esteem, regaining a voice, and minimizing level of fear are what must be done to go from victim to *victor*. When children are involved, they also may experience the same symptoms. It is imperative that they receive additional support and age-appropriate counseling to make sense of it all.

Depending on what the child has seen, their reactions and perspective can be displayed as "disruptive classroom behaviors, increased anxiety, lack of concentration, startled response (unable to deal with loud noises etc.), reserved or timid personalities, episodes of angry outburst or rage, inability to regulate emotions, and physical aggression." If not properly identified and addressed, this may become a pattern of future behaviors that label them and decrease their ability to be emotionally stable and successful in life.

4

Life After Death
New Life, New Dreams, New Me!

Finding God and Myself Again and Healing

NOW DIVORCED, IT was time for the next chapters of my life
to unfold. The torment continued periodically, but I was
able to build up enough strength and set enough boundaries to keep myself focused. I wanted the misery to end,
and I knew that it was up to me to make it happen. I continued to question how my life ended up less than what
I had imagined, going through phases of depression as I
looked back on all the time I felt I had lost. Lost time, lost
happiness, and lost dreams of having a good husband and
another child began to plague my mind. But I learned that
I had to move past that. The more I focused on the negative, I would miss out on the positive. There was still hope
of me meeting someone new who would truly love me; and

even if I didn't have another child, I had Sadie, who is the best part of me.

With those thoughts to guide me, I began to reinvent myself. By reinventing myself, I began to really seek God in my life. For me, this was truly how I made it through. I had gotten past the "if God loved me, he wouldn't have let me go through this" or the "God is punishing me for the mistakes that I made." I began to have a new perspective on the situation and on my life. I began to look and realize that some of my decisions caused my tragedies and that all could have been worse at any time. I began to see similar situations on television and say thank-you that although my situation was bad, I'm still here. I am a *victor* and not a *victim*.

As I became stronger, I began new endeavors and focused on a better life for Sadie and me. However, during this time of my healing, I neglected to realize how much Sadie had gone through. Because she was so young at the time, it didn't seem that she would be affected, but she was. Once I gained clarity, I focused on helping Sadie heal.

Sadie, at this time, was about four. Most days, she was full of smiles; but occasionally, her face was full of frowns and anger. I began to notice that if I would say things to her and she either did not like it or disagreed with it, she had an enraged look on her face. Other times, she would bump into me, expressing that it was "not on purpose." However, she did it frequently, and many times with the same angered and infuriated facial expression that I mentioned above. Over time, this became more and more frequent, and ultimately, I realized that she had been angry with me.

Children don't always verbalize their hurt and pain, but they will act it out. It was at this time that I realized how much the situation we lived through affected her. Although she was not visually present in all the incidents that happened, significant effects from the ones she had seen made an impact on her. Her emotions became a roller coaster, and she had a heightened sense of anxiety and fear.

Now realizing this, I began to talk with Sadie and tried to help her understand the new life we had. And although she was just the young age of four, she was able to express to me the hurt she had felt. I was under the impression that she was upset that her father and I were no longer together. However, she expressed that she actually understood. She knew that we argued a lot, and although she wanted us to be together, she was okay that we weren't. Her biggest anger and upset was feeling as though I left her. "What do you mean?" I asked her. "You live with me now." What I didn't realize was that it was about the separation phase, during which she stayed with her father for a few days at a time to finish school in the neighborhood that we lived in. She had a few overnights during the week due to my work schedule.

You see, I wanted her to still have a father in her life, and Otis's frustration was geared toward me for the most part, so I felt that she would be safe with him. However, I never thought that she would feel like I left her. I began to talk with Sadie and said, "I didn't leave you. When I left, I took you with me." She then said, "But, Mommy, all my stuff [toys, clothing, etc.] was at Daddy's house, and I had to stay at his house without you." I had neglected to realize that most of the bond she created was with me, and she missed the things we did together when I was no longer in the home. Although she was with me most of the time, those moments having to be away from me tormented her. Because of that, she took it out on me through her behaviors.

In time, Sadie was able to stay with just me, and the behaviors began to subside. She had visitation with her father, and she felt better to spend time during just the day doing activities. Once that was settled, I began to notice something else. She had anxiety, and her emotions were all over the place. Her emotions seemed very intense at times, and she could not always control them. Little things would make her cry hysterically, and other times, she would become upset unnecessarily. I then realized that because of the trauma in the house, we either *looked* happy or were angry and upset. She didn't know what to do with her emotions; she never truly learned how to handle them based on what she saw. So now I was at a point where I had to help her with her emotions while I was still dealing with my own.

I also noticed that she began to have similar PTSD symptoms as well. She was emotionally sensitive. Loud sounds startled her. Arguing and screaming of any kind annoyed her, and she never truly felt safe. She also had a hard time if I became sad or upset in any way. I tried not to cry in front of her because I realized that it scared her into thinking that something was wrong with me—just like she would come to console me prior, making sure that I was not hurt and wishing for me to "be okay."

My four-year-old was growing up too fast because of our situation, and I had to regain being her protector and comforter. There was much work to be done for both of us to gain a sense of new normalcy. Part of Sadie being able to heal was being given the time to ask questions about what happened. For so long, she had suppressed most of the memories from her childhood. Now that she had the ability to talk freely about it, she became more relaxed and less anxious. The life we had was damaging, but we had now moved forward. It is an ongoing process, and we will gain strength with each new step we take. It's been almost four years, but we will be whole again.

Reflections

Trauma of any kind can have a lasting effect on the individuals involved. However, when children are involved, the trauma is worse. Not only are you dealing with your emotions, but you have to deal with theirs. They take their cues from you. How you handle your recovery can determine how they deal with theirs now and in the future. Seek additional supports and therapy to assist through this process. Never think a child is not affected just because they don't verbalize it. Look for the cues and signs of depression that may set in as a result. Things to look for are self-isolation, mood swings, irritability, acting-out behaviors, difficulty concentrating, and overall sadness.

Earnest

New Life and God's Grace

So it has been twenty-five years since this journey began. I have lived an experience I had never imagined, but I made it through. I know that there is still a plan for my life and that goodness awaits Sadie and me. Our best days are in front of us, and our worst days are behind. I don't know what the future holds, but I know who holds our future. I am focused on Sadie and believe that what we endured was not in vain. We are survivors and will continue to move in that direction!

Life continues, and the next part of our journey has begun. We are looking forward to all that it has to offer and have been shifted to new places and have met new people. As for me personally, my heart has opened to love again and to be loved. I long to be married and desire a healthy relationship with the right person—someone who loves Sadie and me, is committed to us, understands us, won't harm us, will pray with and for us, and truly loves us unconditionally. With that thought in the back of my mind, I have settled into what I consider to be my "temporary role" as a single mom. In time, all will fall into place; and I believe that when it does, it will be more than we could ever imagine it to be.

Moving forward in strength and gaining a voice, I began to realize many things. Although this is not the course that I would have chosen for my life, I am now able to connect and relate to others in ways I would not have been able to had I not gone through what I have. Through this journey, I am now able to relate to those who have experienced abuse, severe depression with suicidal thoughts, along with those who struggle with being a single mom. I am also more sensitive to signs of abuse and more in tuned with the effects that certain relationships and experiences have on children. Looking back, I learned a lot and now have a different perspective on life and others. Viewing things in a new way has allowed me to make more sense of all that I had to endure.

Sadie and I are cultivating our relationship and continue to work on being whole. We are active in church and spend time together. I make sure to keep her involved in activities and help her to enjoy life. Her emotional needs are also important, and talking through them has eased the unbalance. I am also growing in my career, and things are seemingly falling into place. There is a sense of peace, and we are becoming more settled. With this new sense of peace, I am reminded of a scripture that lets me know my best days are in front of me: "'For I know the plans I have for you,' declares the Lord, 'plans to prosper you and not to harm you, plans to give you hope and a future'" (Jer. 29:11, NIV).

So who is Earnest? Well, Earnest Thompson is the newest and one of the most wonderful additions to this journey. He came into my life when I least expected it and has opened my heart to love again. We had known each other for some time, and he finally asked me out on a date. Our first date was to a basketball game, and we took Sadie. His embracing of her in and of itself made a significant statement to me. In the car ride to the game, I felt an unexplainable peace. Once we were inside, I watched as he cared for Sadie as his own, taking her to the concession stands and just being like a dad to her. I sat in awe as I watched them connect. I remember looking at the two of them and just thinking, "These are my two, I can see my new future." Since that time, we have grown closer and closer, and he has become a significant part of our lives.

Earnest is compassionate, caring, and loving—not to mention handsome, and smart. In him, I feel safe and secure. I have not only opened my heart but my trust again. I have shared some of my hurts and pains with him, and he has helped me with the residue and remnants that continue to resurface from time to time.

Through Earnest, I realized that I was not as healed as I had thought. I was still broken, although I felt strong. He continues to help me deal with the pain of my past and does not allow me to be a victim. He reminds me that I am a victor and that God has more in store for me. He prays for and with me and pushes me to be better. He sees the potential in me and in my life and won't let me give up. He has also embraced Sadie and treats her as his own. Since Earnest became a part of our lives, I have noticed the changes in both me and in Sadie. I don't know where this new journey will take us, but I am ready for the next part of it to be the best part. Earnest, thank you for helping this woman, who was once broken, continue to heal. I am excited for all God has in store for us and the future.

It has been a long journey, and it is not over. It is one that has taught me a great deal about life. I am stronger because of it, and I am reminded that I will continue to make it through by the grace of God. What's next on this journey, I don't know. But I know that things can only get better from here. Through my journey, I pray you have found strength in yours. Never give up on you and know that you are not alone. Pray and seek sound counsel and information. Talk to someone you trust. Remember safety in all that you choose to do in your situation. I love you all. Stand strong.

Reflection

When you have been through difficulties, it's easy to lose hope and feel as though life is becoming desolate. However, as you go through your healing process, you learn that you are stronger than you ever imagined you could be. There will always be a remnant of the past pain I endured. I, however, no longer allow it to hold me from who I know that I am and who I know I can be. Knowing this has allowed me to open my heart again, expecting the best because I've been through the worst. God's grace is alive for me.

5

Letters from Sasha and Education

Letters from Sasha

*Trust in the Lord with your whole heart and lean
not to your own understanding, in all your ways
acknowledge him and he will direct your path.*

—Proverbs 3:5–6

To Those Experiencing the Violence

I UNDERSTAND YOUR pain and your fears. You wondered how
you ended up in this place in your life, and it is not easy. But
know that you are not alone. God still has a plan for you
to see your way clear. Remind yourself that you are worth
loving, no matter the situation. It is my prayer that you will

gain the strength that you need to have a voice again. Be safe and find someone you can trust to talk to.

To Those Who Are Family Members

Your family member needs your support and love. Being in this situation is not as clear-cut as it seems. Your loved one needs your understanding and to know that you are there for them when they need you. The hardest thing to do for someone in this situation is to leave. The extreme feelings of fear, guilt, and self-doubt paralyze the power needed to take that step. Be supportive and proceed with caution, remembering that each situation is different. Pray for them and their situation. Do what you are able to and show as much love as you can. Don't give up on them. They need you.

To Those Who Have Used Anger and Control to Feel Loved, Appreciated, and Respected

It has never been God's plan for love to be forced. I am not sure what you have experienced in your life or who has done you wrong, but love is something that is freely given. This type of fear brings false love, false respect, and false appreciation. If this is something you have learned from your past, begin to learn a new way. The steps you choose to take now will last for generations to come.

Work out your frustrations in a healthier way and look at receiving help as a way to make a stride in a new direction. It may be hard to break old habits, but if you do, you will be a part of the solution. You have brokenness inside you that only God and wise counsel can truly heal. Seek a new way to love.

Education and Resources

Education on Abuse

Sasha's story is a story shared by many and can happen to anyone of any age, race, or economic bracket. As you have seen on this journey, abuse has many forms and affects all who are involved. Most abuse starts out as verbal or mental, which ultimately distorts the truth of the situation. By this point, a person is so far into the relationship that they rationalize the abuse by saying things like, "It was just once," "It won't happen again," "I know deep down he really loves me," etc.

Fear and isolation are the key factors of domestic violence that assist in the prolonged thoughts and rationalization to stay. There is fear of increased danger, fear that "no one else can love me," fear that "I can't make it on my own because I don't have the means to sustain myself," or fear that leaving will cause further harm to the family (although the abuse is more harmful). The more isolated a person becomes, the less support they receive and the more fear the abuser can inflict. Isolation assists in the ability to create a world based on the thoughts and ideas of one person, increasing the level of fear. This perpetuates the thoughts that "if I tell someone, it will get worse."

Many look at individuals in this situation and say, "Why don't they just leave?" Most people say, "If a person puts their hands on me, I'm out!" Well, as you've read on this journey, it's not that easy. The mental anguish, manipulation, and fear deplete a person, and they become weakened and lose a sense of identity even before the physical abuse occurs. If there are children involved, the situation becomes even worse. Staying has a negative lasting effect, and leaving can be seen as deadly.

On the pages that follow, you will see the cycles of abuse, the thoughts and feelings related to abuse, and resources of help.

Domestic Violence Research and Informational[1]

SIGNS THAT YOU MAY BE IN AN ABUSIVE RELATIONSHIP

Your Thoughts and Feelings	Actions done by the person you're a relationship with
Do you:	**Does your partner:**
Feeling afraid of your partner much of the time?	Humiliates or yells at you?
Avoiding of certain topics out of fear of angering your partner?	Criticizes you and put you down?
Feel that you can't do anything right for your partner?	Treat you so badly that you're embarrassed for your friends or family to see?
Believe that you deserve to be hurt or mistreated?	Ignore or put down your opinions or accomplishments?

---

[1] "Domestic Violence and Abuse," Help Guide, http://www. helpguide.org/mental/domestic_violence_abuse_types_ signs_causes_effects.htm

SIGNS THAT YOU MAY BE IN AN ABUSIVE RELATIONSHIP

Wonder if you're the one who is crazy?

Blame you for their own abusive behavior?

Feel emotionally numb or helpless?

See you as property or a sex object, rather than as a person?

Your Partner's Violent Behavior or Threats

Your Partner's Controlling Behavior

Does your partner:

Does your partner:

Have a bad and unpredictable temper?

Act excessively jealous and possessive?

Hurt you, or threaten to hurt or kill you?

Control where you go or what you do?

Threaten to take your children away or harm them?

Keep you from seeing your friends or family?

Threaten to commit suicide if you leave?

Limit your access to money, the phone, or the car?

Force you to have sex?

SIGNS THAT YOU MAY BE IN AN ABUSIVE RELATIONSHIP

Destroy your belongings?   Constantly check up on you?

(http://www.helpguide.org/mental/domestic_violence_abuse_types_signs_causes_effects.htm)

Types of Domestic Violence[2]

Physical: Inflicting or attempting to inflict physical injury

Example: grabbing, pinching, shoving, slapping, hitting, biting, arm-twisting, kicking, punching, hitting with blunt objects, stabbing, shooting

Withholding access to resources necessary to maintain health

Example: medication, medical care, wheelchair, food or fluids, sleep, hygienic assistance forcing alcohol or other drug use

---

[2] "Domestic Violence: Finding Safety and Support—Understanding the Problem," New York State, accessed May 18, 2015, http://www.opdv.ny.gov/help/fss/theproblem.html

Sexual: Coercing or attempting to coerce any sexual contact without consent

Example: marital rape, acquaintance rape, forced sex after physical beating, attacks on the sexual parts of the body, forced prostitution, fondling, sodomy, sex with others. Attempting to undermine the victim's sexuality by treating him/her in a sexually derogatory manner, criticizing sexual performance and desirability, accusations of infidelity, withholding sex.

Psychological: Instilling or attempting to instill fear

Example: intimidation, threatening physical harm to self, victim, and/or others, threatening to harm and/or kidnap children, menacing, blackmail, harassment, destruction of pets and property, mind games, stalking

Isolating or attempting to isolate victim from friends, family, school, and/or work

Example: withholding access to phone and/or transportation, undermining victim's personal relationships, harassing others, constant "checking up," constant accompaniment, use of unfounded accusations, forced imprisonment

Emotional: Undermining or attempting to undermine victim sense of worth

Example: constant criticism, belittling victim's abilities and competency, name-calling, insults, put-downs, silent treatment, manipulating victim's feelings and emotions to induce guilt, subverting a partner's relationship with the children, repeatedly making and breaking promises

Economic: Making or attempting to make the victim financially dependent

Example: maintaining total control over financial resources including victim's earned income or resources received through public assistance or social security, withholding money and/or access to money, forbidding attendance at school, forbidding employment, on-the-job harassment, requiring accountability and justification for all money spent, forced welfare fraud, withholding information about family running up bills for which the victim is responsible for payment

The Cycle of Abuse[3]

The Full Cycle of Domestic Violence: An Example

The emphasis on the following selection are mine. Some variations are made with the names and language for publishing purposes.

> Erwin abuses Martha. After he hits her, he experiences *self-directed guilt*. He says, "I'm sorry for hurting you." What he does not say is, "Because I might get caught." He then *rationalizes his behavior* by saying that Martha is having an affair with someone (whether true or not). He tells her "If you weren't so worthless, I wouldn't have to hit you." He then *acts remorseful*, reassuring her that he will not hurt her again. He then *fantasizes* and reflects on past abuse and how he will not hurt her again. He plans on telling her to go to the store to get some groceries. What he withholds from her is that she has a certain amount of time to do the shopping. When she is held up in traffic and is a few minutes late, he

---

3   "Domestic Violence and Abuse," Help Guide, http://www.helpguide.org/mental/domestic_violence_abuse_types_signs_causes_effects.htm

feels completely justified in assaulting her because "you're having an affair with the store clerk." He has just *set her up*. (Mid-Valley Women's Crisis Service)

- Abuse—Your abusive partner lashes out with aggressive, belittling, or violent behavior. The abuse is a power play designed to show you "who is boss."
- Guilt—After abusing you, your partner feels guilt, but not over what he's done. He's more worried about the possibility of being caught and facing consequences for his abusive behavior.
- Excuses—Your abuser rationalizes what he or she has done. The person may come up with a string of excuses or blame you for the abusive behavior—anything to avoid taking responsibility.
- "Normal" behavior—The abuser does everything he can to regain control and keep the victim in the relationship. He may act as if nothing has happened, or he may turn on the charm. This peaceful honeymoon phase may give the victim hope that the abuser has really changed this time.
- Fantasy and planning—Your abuser begins to fantasize about abusing you again. He spends a lot of time thinking about what you've done wrong and how he'll make you pay. Then he makes a plan for turning the fantasy of abuse into reality.

- Set-up—Your abuser sets you up and puts his plan in motion, creating a situation where he can justify abusing you.

Some Resources and Assistance

- National Domestic Violence (servicing all fifty states, 24-7 assistance)
  1-800-799-SAFE (7233) or 1-800-787-3224 (TTY)
  http://www.thehotline.org
- Safe Horizon's Domestic Violence (servicing New York)
  800-621-HOPE (4673)
  http://www.safehorizon.org/page/call-our-hotlines-9.html
- National Coalition Against Domestic Violence (servicing North Carolina)
  (303) 839-1852
  http://www.ncadv.org/

Book Reviews

I love it! Great read! Very informative and heart wrenching. The trials, struggles, victories, and defeats—but most importantly how to overcome! Resources at the end of the book are great. I think you did an awesome job, and this book will serve as not only a testimony but will be a blessing to many.

———

Love the ending! You tied it together beautifully, and it shows that the story is not over—there is continual growth, repair, and love to be had. It shows that the journey is lengthy, but well worth it.

CPSIA information can be obtained
at www.ICGtesting.com
Printed in the USA
LVOW12s2353300616

494819LV00014B/79/P